Hansel

Retold by Margaret Nash

Illustrated by Kareen Taylerson

Heinemann

Chapter 1

Once upon a time there was a poor woodcutter who had two children called Hansel and Gretel. The woodcutter was a kind father. But the children's stepmother was not so kind.
She did not like Hansel and Gretel at all. Not one little bit.

One day the woodcutter said to his wife,
'What can we do? We have no money
and not much food.'
'Then we will have to send the children
away,' said his wife.
'Oh no, never,' said the woodcutter.
But day after day his wife went on at
him until he said yes.

That night Hansel heard his stepmother say to his father, 'We will have to take the children into the forest and leave them there.'

So Hansel got out of bed and went quietly into the garden. He put lots of little white stones in his pocket.

The next day, before the sun came up, the stepmother woke Hansel and Gretel. 'Get up,' she said. 'We're taking you to work with us in the forest today.' She gave them some crusts of bread.

Off they went into the forest.
Soon they stopped and made a fire.
'Sit by the fire and eat your bread,'
said the stepmother. 'Your father is
going to chop some wood and I am going
with him. We will come back for you at
the end of the day.'

Hansel and Gretel were so tired that they fell asleep. They slept and slept.
The sun went down.
The moon came up.
When Gretel woke up she saw that it was night. She woke up Hansel.
'Oh Hansel,' she said, 'no one has come back for us.'
'Don't worry,' said Hansel, 'we'll find our way back. I made a path of stones. We can follow it home.'

So Hansel and Gretel followed the path of white stones all the way home.

Their father was happy to see them but their stepmother was cross.

'In the morning you will come with us to chop more wood,' she said.

Chapter 2

That night Hansel tried to go out to get some more white stones but he could not open the door.

'Oh well,' he said, 'I will have to make a path of breadcrumbs for us to follow.'

The next day, before the sun came up, the stepmother woke Hansel and Gretel. 'Get up,' she said. 'It's time to go to the forest.'
She gave them some crusts of bread.

This time they went deep into the forest. They walked until the trees were so tall that Hansel and Gretel could not see any sky. Deeper and deeper they went until they could not hear any birds singing.

Then they stopped and made a fire.
'Sit by the fire and eat your bread,'
said the stepmother. 'Your father is
going to chop some wood and I am going
with him. We will come back for you
at the end of the day.'

Hansel and Gretel were so tired that they fell asleep. They slept and slept. The sun went down.
The moon came up.
When Gretel woke she saw that it was night. She woke up Hansel.
'Oh Hansel,' she said, 'no one has come back for us.'
'Don't worry,' said Hansel, 'we'll find our way back. I made a path of breadcrumbs for us to follow.'

Hansel and Gretel looked for the breadcrumbs. But they were not there.
'The birds must have eaten them,' said Gretel sadly.
'We'll just have to find our own way,' said Hansel.
So the two children walked on and on but they couldn't find their way home.

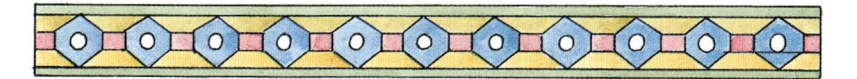

Chapter 3

Then they saw a little house. Hansel and Gretel ran up to it.

'Oh look, Hansel,' said Gretel, 'this little house is made of gingerbread. It's made of sweets too. And its windows are made of sugar.'

Just then the door opened and an old woman came out.

'Come in, children, come in,' she said. 'I won't hurt you.'

She sat Hansel and Gretel at a table and gave them pancakes and milk. Then she showed them two little beds with white sheets. That night Hansel and Gretel slept in the two little beds as happy as could be.

But the next day when the children woke up, the old woman took Hansel outside and put him in a cage.

'You are going to stay here until you're fat, then I'm going to eat you,' she said.

'Oh no,' Gretel cried out.

She tried to open the cage but she could not.

Every day the old woman made Gretel take food to Hansel.

'I want him fat,' she would shout. 'Do you hear? Fat, fat, fat!'

And every day, when Hansel had eaten his food, the old woman told him to put his little finger out of the cage so that she could see how fat it was. But the old woman could not see very well, so Hansel did not put out his finger. He put out a chicken bone.

19

Soon the old woman grew tired of waiting for Hansel to get fat.

'I am going to eat him today, even if he isn't fat,' she told Gretel.

The old woman lit the oven. She waited until it was hot.

'Get in there, Gretel,' said the old woman. 'Tell me if the oven is ready. Go on, get in.'

But Gretel was very clever. She knew what the old woman was going to do so she said, 'You'll have to show me how to.' When the old woman put her head in the oven, Gretel gave her a big push and shut the oven door.

'That's the end of you,' said Gretel.

Gretel ran out of the house.

'Hansel, Hansel!' she shouted. 'I've got rid of the old woman.'

She opened the cage and Hansel jumped out and threw his arms around her.

'Thank you, Gretel,' he said. 'We are safe at last.'

Hansel and Gretel ran back into the house and there, in a corner of the room, they found boxes of jewels.
'Oh Gretel,' said Hansel, 'we will be rich. Just look at all those jewels.'
So they picked up some of the jewels and put them in their pockets, then they ran out of the house and into the forest.

They ran and ran through the trees until at last they saw their father's house. They ran into the house and threw their arms around their father. He was so happy to see them. And as for the stepmother, she had long gone. Hansel and Gretel showed their father all the jewels.

'Now we will be rich, father,' they said.

'And we will all be happy too,' said their father.